Max and the Bird House

Story by Annette Smith
Illustrations by Richard Hoit

Max and Grandad went outside.

"Look at the snow," said Max.
"It's all over the garden."

"It is winter, now, Max,"
said Grandad.
"It will be cold for weeks and weeks."

"The little birds look cold,"
said Max.

"They will be hungry, too,"
said Grandad.
"Let's get some bread
and some nuts."

"Here you are, little birds,"
said Max.

The big cat from next door
jumped up on the fence.

"Oh, no!" said Max.

"The little birds are flying away.
They will not come back
for the bread, now.
Go away, cat!"

The next day,
Max came out with some bread
for the hungry birds.

But the big cat came back.

"Max," said Grandad,
"we can make a bird house.
Will you come and help me?"

Max helped Grandad
make a little house
for the birds.

"This will be a good place
for the bird house," said Grandad.
"The cat will not get the birds
way up here."

The big cat sat on the fence.
It looked at the birds.

The birds went into the little house to eat the bread and the nuts.

"They are safe now," said Max.